Animals Big and Small

Daniel Nunn

Raintree

Chicago, Illinois

www.capstonepub.com
Visit our website to find out more information about Heinemann-Raintree books.

To order:
☎ Phone 800-747-4992
💻 Visit www.capstonepub.com to browse our catalog and order online.

Edited by Daniel Nunn, Rebecca Rissman, and Sian Smith
Designed by Joanna Hinton-Malivoire
Picture research by Elizabeth Alexander
Illustrations by Joanna Hinton-Malivoire
Originated by Capstone Global Library Ltd.
Production by Victoria Fitzgerald

Library of Congress Cataloging-in-Publication Data
Nunn, Daniel.
  Animals big and small / Daniel Nunn.
    p. cm. – (Math every day)
  Includes bibliographical references and index.
  ISBN 978-1-4329-5733-9 (hb) – ISBN 978-1-4329-5738-4 (pb)
  1. Size perception–Juvenile literature. 2. Body size–Juvenile literature. 3. Comparison (Philosophy)–Juvenile literature. I. Title.
  BF299.S5N86 2012
  153.7'52–dc23
                                    2011013021

Acknowledgments
We would like to thank the following for permission to reproduce photographs: iStockphoto p. 14 (© Christian Weibell); Shutterstock pp. 4–5 (© Eric Isselée), 6 left (© Lisa A. Svara), 6 right (© photobac), 7 (© Eric Isselée), 8, 9 right (© joyfull), 9 left (© Gelpi), 10 left (© Christian Musat), 10 right, 11 (© Kletr), 12 right (© Eric Isselée), 12 left (© Sergii Figurnyi), 13 top (© Alexander Ishchenko), 13 bottom (© Eric Isselée), 15 (© Andre Goncalves), 16 (© Galushko Sergey), 17 (© Krzysztof Odziomek), 18 left (© Verena Lüdemann), 18 right (© Michael C. Gray), 19 (© Pichugin Dmitry), 20 (© FloridaStock), 21 (© kurdistan), 22–23 (© Susan Schmitz)

Cover photograph of a chihuahua on the back of a Great Dane reproduced with permission of Getty Images (Brand X Pictures). Back cover photograph of a cat reproduced with permission of Shutterstock (© Eric Isselée); photograph of a mouse Shutterstock (© Sergii Figurnyi).

Every effort has been made to contact copyright holders of any material reproduced in this book. Any omissions will be rectified in subsequent printings if notice is given to the publisher.

Printed in the United States   5657

Contents

Animal Sizes

Let's look at animals.
They are all different sizes.

Whether big, small, or tiny they are full of surprises!

Big and Small

Dog 1 is **big**.

Dog 2 is **small**.

Dog 3 is the **biggest** dog of them all.

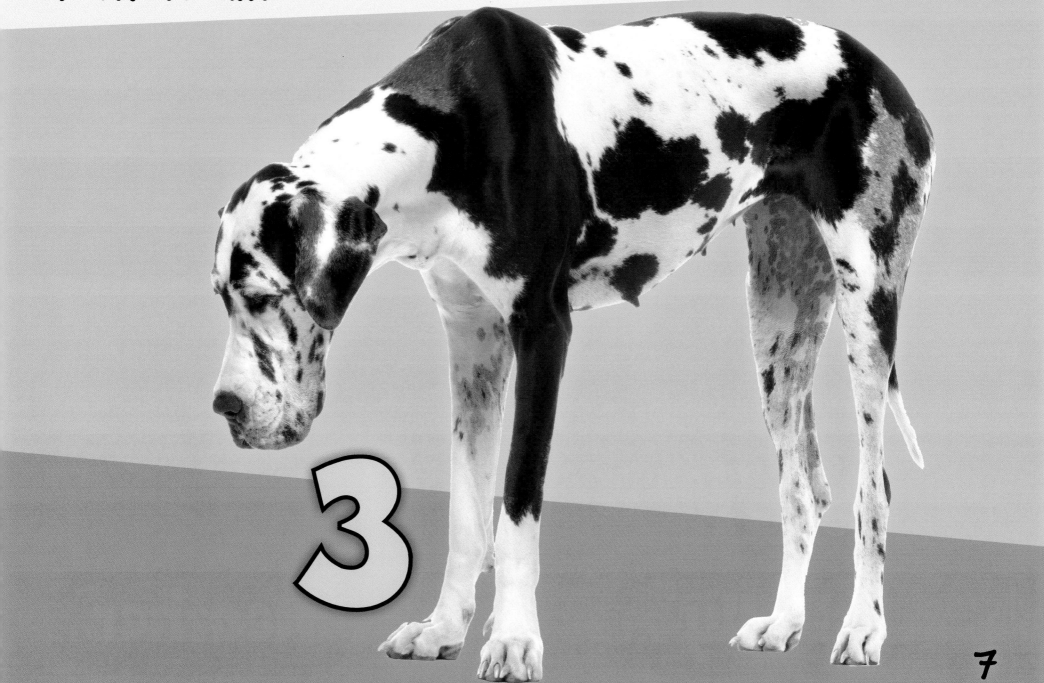

Here are two horses, lined up in a row.

Holly

Heather

Holly

Heather

Is Holly bigger than Heather? Let's see if you know!

9

Tall and Short

Here are two more animals.
Which one is tall?

What about these two?

Which one is shorter,
which one is taller?

13

Long and Short

This snake is long.
It's a bit of a whopper.

This insect is short.
It's a tiny grasshopper.

Under the water, a short orange fish swims by.

A long grey fish swims closer,
it looks like it's saying "Hi!"

Wide and Narrow

This antelope is narrow.

This hippo is **wide**.

You wouldn't have much luck getting a hippo to hide.

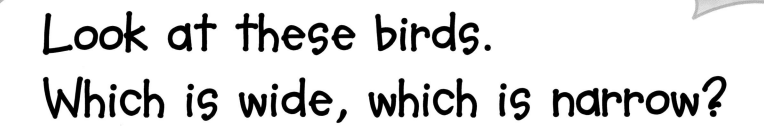

It's easy! The eagle is wider than that tiny sparrow.

sparrow

The Same Size

Which dog is the biggest, or are they all the same size?

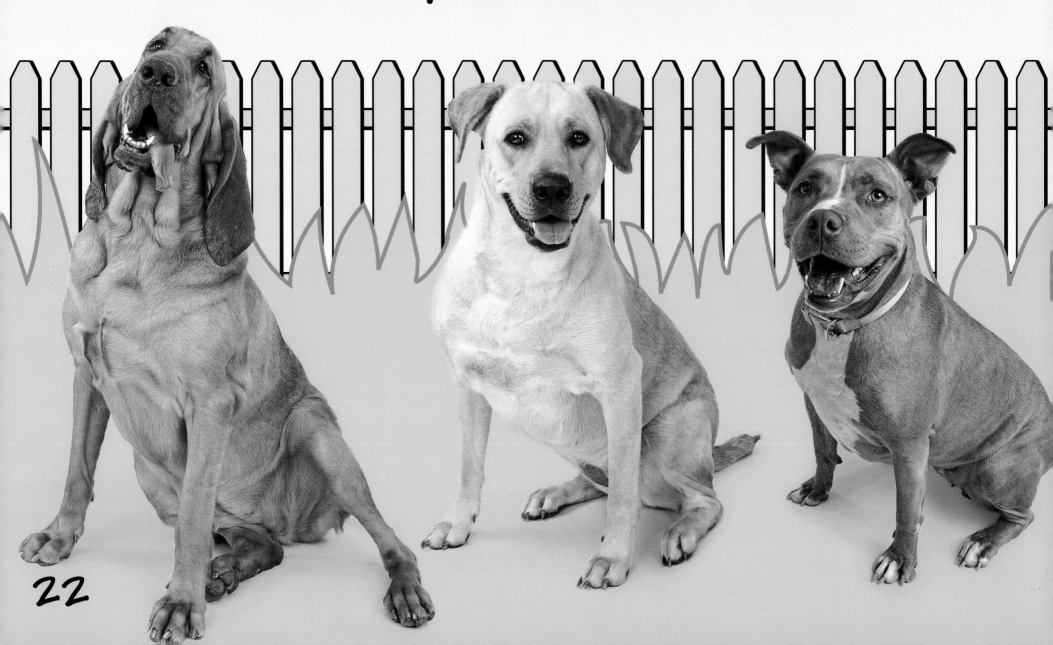

You could use a ruler,
or just use your eyes.

Answer on page 24

Index

Answer to question on page 22

The dogs are all different sizes. The first dog is the biggest dog. It is bigger than all the others.